Preschool up

# Elfin's Adventure

## in Alphabet Town

*by Laura Alden*
*illustrated by Linda Hohag*

created by Wing Park Publishers

**CHILDRENS PRESS ®**
CHICAGO

**Library of Congress Cataloging-in-Publication Data**

Alden, Laura, 1955-
    Elfin's adventure in Alphabet Town / by Laura Alden ;
illustrated by Linda Hohag.
       p.    cm. — (Read around Alphabet Town)
    Summary: Elfin meets "e" words on his adventure in Alphabet
Town. Includes activities.
    ISBN 0-516-05405-8
    [1. Alphabet—Fiction.   2. Elves—Fiction.]   I. Hohag, Linda, ill.
II. Title.   III. Series.
PZ7.A3586El   1992
[E]—dc 20
                                91-20545
                                      CIP
                                       AC
                                     Rev.

# Elfin's *Adventure*

in Alphabet Town

You are now entering Alphabet Town,
With houses from "A" to "Z."
I'm going on an "E" adventure today,
So come along with me.

This is the "E" house of Alphabet
Town. Elfin lives here.

Elfin likes everything that begins
with the letter "e."

Elfin likes

engines.

He has eleven of them.

And Elfin loves his best friend,

Elephant.

The one "e" thing Elfin does not like is eels.

Eek! Elephant does not like eels either.

But Elfin and Elephant both like

eggs,

especially Easter eggs.

"Tomorrow is the Easter egg hunt," Elfin shouted in Elephant's ear one evening. "Easy," said Elephant. "Please do not shout in my ear."

"Sorry," said Elfin more quietly. "But
it is time to visit Easter Bunny."
"Okay," said Elephant.

"I will come along," said

Eagle.

"I like Easter eggs too."

So Elfin hopped on Eagle's back.
They flew high in the evening sky.

Elephant followed them to Easter Bunny's house.

Easter Bunny was busy, coloring eggs and putting them in

Easter baskets.

"Can you help me?" he cried. "I have eight hundred eggs to color."

Elfin liked Easter Bunny. "I will help you," he said.

Eagle and Elephant helped too.
They worked all evening and into
the early morning.

"Now, we must hide the eggs before everyone wakes up in Alphabet Town," said Easter Bunny.

Eagle flew east.
Elephant went west.
Easter Bunny hopped north.
Elfin ran south.

They emptied eighty Easter baskets.
They hid eight hundred eggs.

The sun came up.
There were eggs everywhere.

"Wake up, everyone!" shouted Elfin.
"Wake up! It is Easter!"

Elfin, Elephant and Eagle watched the children hunt eggs until it was

eight o'clock.

Then they hurried over to Easter Bunny's house.

"Now it is time to eat," said Easter Bunny. They all sat down for a breakfast of eggs.

After breakfast, Easter Bunny said,
"Here are some special eggs for my
special helping friends."

And he gave Elephant, Eagle, and Elfin
each an enormous chocolate Easter egg.
"Happy Easter!" he said.

# MORE FUN WITH ELFIN

### What's in a Name?

In my "e" adventure, you read many "e" words. My name begins with an "E." Many of my friends' names begin with "E" too. Here are a few.

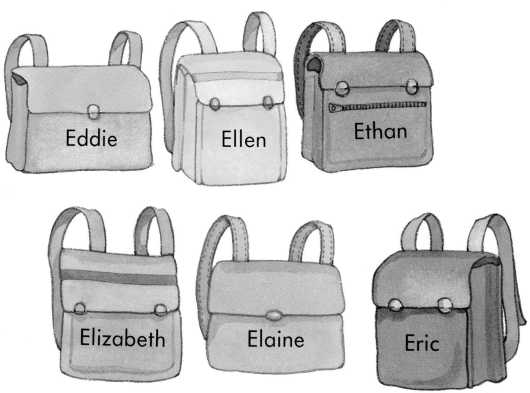

Eddie

Ellen

Ethan

Elizabeth

Elaine

Eric

Do you know other names that start with "E"?
Does your name start with "E"?

## Elfin's Word Hunt

I like to hunt for words with "e" in them. Can you help me find the words on this page that begin with "e"? How many are there?

escalator

elk

bee

ice

doll

deer

earth

bed

Can you find any words with "e" in the middle?
Can you find any with "e" at the end?
Can you find a word with no "e"?

### Elfin's Favorite Things

"E" is my favorite letter. I love "e" things. Can you guess why? You can find some of my favorite "e" things in my house on page 7. How many "e" things can you find there? Can you think of more "e" things?

MY Alphabet Town Dictionary

Now you make up an "e" adventure.